I0817532

DADDY

ALSO BY
JAKE BYRNE

Celebrate Pride with Lockheed Martin

DADDY

JAKE BYRNE

BRICK BOOKS

Library and Archives Canada Cataloguing in Publication

Title: Daddy / Jake Byrne.
Names: Byrne, Jake (Poet), author.
Identifiers: Canadiana (print) 20240403126 | Canadiana (ebook) 20240403207
| ISBN 9781771316408
(softcover) | ISBN 9781771316415 (EPUB) | ISBN 9781771316422 (PDF)
Subjects: LCGFT: Poetry. | LCGFT: Queer poetry.
Classification: LCC PS8603.Y75 D33 2024 | DDC C811/.6—dc23

We gratefully acknowledge the Canada Council for the Arts, the Government of Canada through the Canada Book Fund, and the Ontario Arts Council and the Government of Ontario for their support of our publishing program.

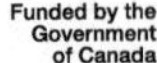

Canada Council for the Arts Conseil des Arts du Canada

Edited by John Barton and River Halen.
Author photo by Liahm Ruest.
The book is set in Calluna and Calder.
Design by Kilby Smith-McGregor.

The cover image depicting Abraham's sacrifice of Isaac (painted c. 1589–1603), is housed in the Piasecka-Johnson Collection in Princeton, New Jersey. It is of contested provenance, thought to be either the work of Caravaggio or Bartolomeo Cavarozzi.

Brick Books
487 King St. W.
Kingston, ON
K7L 2X7

www.brickbooks.ca

Though much of the work of Brick Books takes place on the ancestral lands of the Anishinaabeg, Haudenosaunee, Huron-Wendat, and Mississaugas of the Credit peoples, our editors, authors, and readers from many backgrounds are situated from coast to coast to coast in Canada on the traditional and unceded territories of over six hundred nations who have cared for Turtle Island from time immemorial. While living and working on these lands, we are committed to hearing and returning the rightful imaginative space to the poetries, songs, and stories that have been untold, under-told, wrongly told, and suppressed through colonization.

How long must I wander here
In this final house of my father?

—Audre Lorde, "Martha"

FRED
(angrily)

How'd you get inside my house?

MYSTERY MAN

You invited me.

It is not my custom to go where I am not wanted.

— David Lynch, *Lost Highway*, 30:59 – 31:06

This book is dedicated to the memory of a little cat named My Sweet Princess (2018-2023)

CONTENTS

DADDY

gnostic iambic pre-exposure jockstrap jukebox prophylaxis

DADDY

PARALLEL VOLUMES

The only surprise of my father calling eleven times in a single evening is which unlisted number he'll try next.

I recount this to my therapist without much affect.
I'm sorry, he says.
That must have felt very bad, he says.
How are you feeling right now, as we talk about it?

I am feeling that the vessel of my personhood fills at an intolerable rate.

To paraphrase Dionne Brand, the author is not the *only* person in this body.

We each experience three wounds in life:
the mind, the spirit, and the body.
In that order, if you're lucky.

My favourite book is a television program from Japan called *Neon Genesis Evangelion*.
It's about giant robots and, no matter how hard you try, you can
never truly be known by another human being.
Especially a parent.

But I do try. I try so hard.
That's why I bus to see my therapist mid-winter.
I am seeking his assistance with a complex project.

I need his help untangling these narratives I’ve written for myself.

In Borges's library—via Brand, again—there is a tome that contains me.
It is the sum of every detail, thought, experience, memory,
false memory, illusion, observation, cell, and particle.

Without the bindings of my body.

I intend to either write this book or steal it from the library.

I saw a sun as white as the moon and it terrified me, frankly.
The last time my father called I knew better, but picked up anyway.
Pilot the Eva, Shinji, or Rei will have to do it again.

My father calls to talk about my poems
and seamlessly incorporates my words into his paranoid delusions.
He says I ought to be more careful what I write, implies the poems
come from a demon birthing itself through the vessel of my body.

When I was born, I did not anticipate that I would feel these sorts of feelings.

Roaming the stacks of the universal library, searching for the book of my life.

That is pretty much the entire plot of the book of my life.

My father's too.
That's why he calls so much.

He calls because he believes if he can recite the book of his life
over the telephone he will reach me…

The reason I am interested in writing the book of my life should now be made clear.

When you talk to
a psychotic episode over the phone,
you learn what theorists mean when they call language *infinite*.
How infinite can also mean *zero,* or *nothing*.
The joke reads as sad, because the laughter sounds empty.
This is what poets might call *dramatic irony*.

When I pick up the phone to speak to my father,
I hear infinite combinations, arranged according to a common theme:
the doctor poisons;
the medication sickens;
the remedy is worse than his disease.

If I were to scrawl in the book of my life I would add:
to poison the well is to have any children.

When I conclude the book of my life
I will read it to you, reader.

Just as I'm doing now.
Please hang up the receiver.

YOU CAN CHECK OUT ANYTIME

Writing my poems about DADDY in the library
Only to discover that DADDY is in the library
The same library I go to four days a week
Of all the dysfunctional libraries in this city

It makes sense that he's here—public libraries
Are a place where homeless people
Hang out, generally

Thought to say hello
To walk up and to begin anew
To put myself in DADDY's arms
To weep for the promise
Of new beginnings

But by the time my brain completes the thought
My body has already
Sprinted out the exit

EERIE HONEY

It was a rum-soaked plum cake in my mouth. I stuffed it there
Because my cat was going to eat it. If my cat dies, I do. And he will—
And the name of that day is *EERIE HONEY*. I haven't yet divulged to you
That when I was fourteen I dreamed of carving *PURITY* into my arm
And drinking the liquor that flowed from the cask. I was sickened by dreams,
Fevers, crashing waves of blood sugar...   Better to carve your mother's name
Into your palm: the palms of our hands are so rarely exposed
In conversation.   Why magicians put coins in them.   And the plums were
Ringed in the middle of the sponge, purple and red like blood.
And when a friend saw them, I was too proud, still am too proud, for
There is so much blood I don't know the name of. There is the
Clanging of a bell, a loud fell bell. An Edgar Allan Poe–style bell
In the sacred temple of my brain now clanging as though it were
Inflamed by Sazerac and all the blood I own but cannot name.
It is only life
As we choose to ignore it. Blood is
The one true thing of ours we own and can
Give away. I see the photo of DADDY
Where I look like him
And I touch his face when I touch my own in the mirror.
The same bad choices. I do not know my DADDY's phone number. We haven't spoken in
Eight months at least. I haven't had a drop to drink in seven years
But I am California sober   Which is not sober. Lana playing in the bar
Covered in posters and photographs of forgotten movie stars, dark
Forest-green wood, an ATM, a stink of piss and cigarettes. Me at the ATM again
Buying a round
Then me soaked in my own piss Begging to stay on somebody's couch or mattress
          DADDY
Always knew, always could tell   The shameful stink
Of my hangover. I do not know the   Names of my ancestors.
          But their wounds know me

I am so drunk I have forgotten your name   Does that make me a monster?
     I'm sorry

To be such a bummer when we're   Trying to
Have some fun   In Turkey or in Hungary
          In Madrid, in Tokyo, in Prague
               The youth hostel, in the famous-ruin bar. We are trying to
     have a little fun
And have a little drink or two before therapy. I call it a variation on Negroni.
I find it makes the words pour easily. An Americano
     I am having a martini
Made with sweet vermouth and a piano's glissando
Shaken in a silver jar   In Poland or in Hungary
Ontario or Boston we loved   Just a little cocktail before therapy.
It's been eight months since I spoke to DADDY   And I don't know his number
     Never have   Probably never will. Nobody's spoken to him
In a long long time. But he will be fine. His behaviour is—
Has always been—extremely normal. Never seen him drink.
I love an Americano because they taste of metal   They taste of the blood that is
The EERIE HONEY to billions of
Thirsty humans that predate me.   In my family this
Is normal behaviour
The resolve to never drink again
Resolves itself as everything does
Around the orbit of the sun.   A bar in which
The ATM is right next to the bathroom reeks of piss and
We've all had the most marvellous
Just the most marvellous conversations you could have
In this arena of starlight.   Card games and
Loosened up I let myself become cruel   And we're partying, baby   It's fun and
We're horny with DADDY   It's time for karaoke   I go up to the mic
Twenty-six times, one song for each year of my life   I sing songs of blood, yes
          Songs of the blood of my family   And three or four by Kate Bush
We feel warm and good on the streets of Budapest
          Reeking of Absolut and salmonella   Dylan Thomas's DTs and

Dysentery   Could I still ring my DADDY's number then? Which doctor's office
Is he sleeping in?   How many coins can you skip on the surface of a drink?
How many drinks can you skip   My small-town faggot party trick:
    How many tables can my manhood drink you under?
    We're drinking a cocktail
In sunny Madrid and yes yes   Have a real fun party vibe playing
    Games of blood and drinking and here's one called King's Cup: you play
    a special game of Yahtzee   I swim out   To the middle of the lake   Alone
And wearing all your clothes. But I'm not alone! My sister is there   My
    boyfriend too
To assess how serious this attempt might be.   If you roll Yahtzee! I'll jump
    off the roof
Of the youth hostel and I am in fact   Never alone
You may sharpen that   Into a knife.   I drink or I starve.   I have
To do a lot of bad bad things you may not want to   That's a bottle of vermouth
Pouring out your arm. It is a special occasion and we've broken
Out the champagne.   The sun has completed
Another orbit round the Earth.   DADDY isn't feeling well; he's wearing
His oxygen tank in the sitting room   He won't speak for six months or so
And then blood will pour from his mouth As mead does from sparkling honey
I am seven years old and blow out the Birthday cocktail and watch TV   Perhaps you
Drive through a tree   When the hour is three a.m. and I AM drunk under sunny
    Spanish sun
When life is gay and funny

A POEM ABOUT MY PET CANARY I

Some lessons are best learned the hard way.
All living things
Need food,
Water, a place to sleep
That isn't covered in shit and
Feathers, takeout containers.
Even a bird
Gold as sun
On spring wind.
I wanted him to alight on my hand.
He never did.
I was seven, and for my birthday
Was permitted to choose my own pet
And swore to Mom I'd care for the bird alone.
If I wanted to cage
Warm-throated sunshine, I was
Going to have to work each day to keep it there.

    Light, what it does is move.
It flies. It passes through things.
It doesn't wait for you. It couldn't
If it wanted to.
It sings, but in July
Will require water
Twice a day, at least.
At seven, I had difficulty
Grasping the magnitude
Of my commitment.
The Trojans were merely the *first* ones to learn
That a gift is often synonymous
With a trap

INTIMACY

Children like me
Distract themselves with toys,
Refuse to leave their wooden blocks on vinyl floor,
And do not greet the caregiver
After she returns.

Whoopi Goldberg, on the subject of marriage:

I don't want anybody in my house.

DADDY

All along, the time-consuming lesson was

I—I could love myself, instead!!!

Congratulations—the supporting cast all clap

Confetti through the air   Super Smash Bros. Party Ball   Confetto

Confettitude   Confetticity   A Jell-O cake

Sponge muddy with   Rainbow stripes   My therapy homework:

For three minutes a day place your hand over your heart and sigh loudly

I tried to starve it away   I rooted my lack of control

Into the contours of my flesh   And then I thought

A teenage bright idea: Eliminate it

My first drug of choice was hunger

Second, caffeine   Then nicotine   The latter two, means to enable the first

In this way does suffering accumulate   From cause to effect   Orange
blossom to peel

Nobody tells you   How good hunger can feel

They don't teach that in school   I wonder why!

The first few days at least   Third month?   Bleak

Second year?   Grim   Peanut butter and Nutella sandwiches

Binged on after "unsuccessful" starvation runs   Two days, now three

Reading that Billie Piper, actress, managed to go

Four, five days without food   I thought this something to aspire to

Fevered-sleep hours   After consumption of carbohydrate

Blasted pancreas   Mixed deluxe nuts   Whittling myself down

To the least repulsive number I could bear

That number crawling ever lower

The taste of diet soda   The taste of black coffee

Three no-cal sweeteners   Three days without   I never got to four

The taste of digesting nothing but the roof of my own mouth

The support on offer an occasional passive-aggressive   *Honey*

No one should ever be that thin

The taste of my mother's denial

About her own tendencies   How those could be passed

As though through placenta, from mother to son   Like blood

One day Ali said to me   *She has an anorexic's cruelty*

The taste of control hollowed of my bones

The period of my life I saw DADDY every week

And every week we ate at the same restaurant—Swiss Chalet

Because their food "didn't contain pesticides" I was too young to recognize

The delusion But not too young to know Something weird

Was happening O Swiss Chalet I loved you once

I smell your Swiss Chalet sauce I puke it up

I didn't want to hang out with *any* parent

Let alone DADDY

DADDY's an entrepreneur With some unusual business ideas...

Anger, paranoia, mysterious burnouts The interrogations

He'd remember Some facial expression as evidence

I was conspiring against him The threats of lawsuits against my family

The phone calls from foreign doctors' offices

This is a list poem, I suppose A list of grievances I wrote around for many years

The car the car The fucking car

Filled up to my knees with garbage

Driving with his feet   Locking me inside
While he slept on the shoulder of the Gardiner

Staring out the window of the car while he talked   At me

Wanting to escape into the scenery   How I never called him Father

As he demanded   Berated   Wasn't DADDY

DADDY was DADDY, not him

The taste of everyone pretending   This was normal

The feeling I was a vessel he was trying to fill

With poison.

And yet

And yet...

Despite it all

Despite what I could say   In words

In images   Or in their absences

According to   My biased   Powers of recollection

My ability to rearrange these powers
Into a pleasing form in words
Despite my own best efforts
I find I do love

My domineering   Creative   Profoundly self-absorbed
Human   Very very sick   DADDY

In many ways

He tried his very best

Everyone was doing their very best

Their very best did not suffice

My very best has always been

In reading the room

Subtle shifts in the mood

And tone of voice of the adults around me

Scanning for threats

And suppressing my needs

To perform any role I'm required to, flawlessly

Smiling through scrutiny

Until my work's done

And I get a gold star

And the room shifts again, and no one is hostile or angry

Then I can leave and go back to hide

In my books, my video games, drugs, or my fantasies

Before another change in vibe announces

A new role will be required of me And quickly

Sometimes the role
Is that of a horse that needs breaking

If that was your childhood

Who do you think you might grow up to be?

You grow up to be a performer, of course

You grow up to be someone who believes

To receive love, you must first demonstrate you deserve it

Chasing little gold stars all over the place

From anybody who might have one

No matter how many you get

You feel empty

Or I did, at least.

But I am pleased to report
Those beliefs about love
Were incorrect, based on a fiction

And that there were other fun
And healing pastimes
I could apply my training to

A career in art, perhaps

Or

Being DADDY's Eager BOY

Always be happy and

Cheerful and free

To demonstrate

Exactly how much Of another man

I can contort myself

To fit inside me

ABUNDANCE OF QUALITY WE MIGHT CALL MATERNAL

What I want to think of when I think of "mother"
is this: endlessly giving, cornucopia of fruits,
a child's sensation of a hug. But I cannot go back there.
Not for all the casseroles or clouds of great aunts
bathed in Opium.
        Opium, too, does not suffice,
                not that I've ever had the real shit,
        captures the warmth of feeling
but no actual safety or security.
I want to put something of motherhood in the poem.
I want to put something of motherhood inside my heart.
To give my partner a tender kiss when he hasn't
showered in a week. To be abundant. To overflow.
But I can't give what I don't know. The gift
my mother gave me was her fear.
I keep it in a silver cup, overfull with tears.

PORTION

I weighed out
an ounce of food
onto a matte black digital scale
I ought not permit myself to keep.

In times of chaos, many seek comfort
in control.

Ritual, routine, restriction, reverence:
there are many ways to cultivate
discipline.

Those that involve punishment are merely closer to hand.

The image in the mirror comes from the kingdom of false dreams.

I know I have received only one true dream thus far.

I weigh self-compassion
against the hunk of fool's gold
my father gave me when I was six.

One of these things is too weighty to bear.

As much as I weighed
the same year my aunt
held me on her lap, said,
Look at these
belly rolls you've got,
the same year
I started sucking in.

GAMES NIGHT!!!

Games were the only way
I could wield my anger against DADDY
Who'd clean my clock
At chess
      Risk the rare time
He'd permit himself show
                  His sadism openly
                  Acceptably

I have observed that GAMES NIGHT!!!
Is often a valve
Releasing the steam of
Unpermitted emotions
Such as aggression
In the kind of
Happy family that
Looks an awful lot like mine
Trivial pursuits lead to feuds and blows

The only game I'd match DADDY in was Boggle
So we'd play every week, win percentages oscillating
Between forty-nine and fifty-one
My grandparents would join
But in this contest were fifth business, NPCs
Furious I studied
To overcome him

I challenged my partner to a game
On our second date, Strip Boggle in his rented attic
Only to discover that
Sometimes winning isn't fun

Closing the plastic case
Every stitch of his clothes on the busted hardwood
Me as covered with my shame as ever:

G-O   W-I-N   W-I-N-S
B-A-D

S-O-N   I-S   S-A-D
D-E-A-D
D-A-D-S

PIETÀ

Mom tries to get me off the phone
in under sixty seconds every time I call.
I don't have time to feel the feelings I might need to feel today.
I pay my therapist to listen to my bullshit and cut through it
like a brick of factory-farmed cheese.
He does, a little too
effectively
for my ego's satisfaction.

Where does that ego live
inside the body?
The back of the neck:
hot, flushed, tight.

Where mother cat
would nip her kit
before she rips
the mats out of its fur.

My therapist asks if I feel lonely
and if I'd like to cry.

I do.

And I would like to, but cannot.

In shades of blue flannel pyjamas
I remember *discipline* the euphemism.

I remember her remorse afterward
and the feeling that I needed to comfort her
and not the other way around.

Euphemism: *beautiful speech.*

THE LORD OF LOSS IN PLEASURE

It is always past the hour
where the past can be retrieved,
yet never late enough
that we cannot begin again.
When my grandfather and I
played chess, I'd bring
a book to read between his moves.
I'd see him see the board, the lamplight
reflecting off his shiny head
containing thousands of formulae,
every possibility mapped out
and quantified ahead of time.
Ten minutes per deliberation.
I'd shut my book, dog-ear the page,
move my queen to where felt good,
take his bishop, then pick up the book again.
I don't possess his aptitude for math
or perfect pitch, his involuntary
synaesthetic pairing of musical notes
with colours.
In present day, his heart and legs are weak.
I barely read, I don't play chess.
The last time we went to the theatre together
is the last time we'll ever go to the theatre together.
And I think about how I hailed him a taxi,
and the snow was falling round us as
quiet as a library,
and how it made me sad—
that he trudged through the snowbank
on his bad leg, that he
did not steady himself
against my newfound strength,
he did not turn
to take my outstretched hand.

WHAT ARE YOU FRIGHTENED OF?

It can't be *alone.*
That is the *core belief.*

Core. The fun parts
Of the apple nibbled away,
With only what
Is rigid and inflexible
Remaining. A human being
Could chew and swallow about two
Hundred apple seeds
Before the hydrogen cyanide
Contained in them
Deprived the eater
Of the means to live.

No good answer for why
Anybody'd eat that many.

Fibrous pills of
Poison planted
Sprout new life.

Open your mouth.
Swallow hard.

II OF RODS

Some of us are harmed by Mommy

Some of us are harmed by DADDY

No one makes it out of life alive

When DADDY receives divine instructions
You know to be incorrect
When you encounter the fact
That the world is unjust

For the first but not the final time
You will learn you cannot trust your thoughts, your feelings, your emotions
When Mommy and DADDY make you feel bad
Though you think it is their duty

To love and shelter and protect you
They must be right
That must be how it should be
You will learn to disregard the messages of your body

Until the mailbox explodes
Like in that Ashton Kusher movie
That isn't very good

Your certainty is what divides us, DADDY

It is my doubt that sustained me

The policeman DADDY lays down law
Children should be seen
To be happy
Smiling in public makes one happy family

I do so want to be good
Be told I'm a good boy
Being good protects me
And protects my family

If I follow the law to the letter
Shall I earn life's favour?

A baby is born between shadow and crevice

The baby cries out for the touch of a hand

The hand delivers the sting of authority

A man doles out; a boy receives

Splitting between black and white

I have not resolved my DADDY issues

I bring them to my bed to sleep with

Not terribly uncommon, is it

One DADDY is policeman wielding a club
One DADDY is homeless, sleeps under the stars
Both stand on top of me

Sometimes my arms bend back

The Policeman DADDY and the Vagrant DADDY
The Policeman DADDY brings the law
Can see the good or evil of the world inside all things
Except the happy home with damask wallpaper

Policeman DADDY wields care in the form of a big stick
A dividing line to orient the world by
Force in the form of a rod unspoiled
A thick hard cock in the face

Or the song of a throat
That's been washed out with soap

You will know you have
Done something wrong
By the way their eyes change quickly

Policeman DADDY chases Vagrant DADDY
Sleeping under stars or underpasses
Dreaming the secret nature of all things
So perfected and exact

The dream becomes substance, as it does
In *Final Fantasy X*
This stupid video game from 2001

Like a *Spy vs Spy* cartoon
DADDY vs DADDY
Cruel and comical contractions
Which one shall destroy the other

To win dominance over
Which vision of the rotting world
The boy's eyes will grow and learn to see

The boy makes a choice between cruel and crazy

DADDY earns the love of the boy
The boy who let himself be bound
His neck sweetly laid upon
A kindling pyre in the mountains of Moriah
Who'd sweetly let his blood for thee
The boy who'd longed to know the secret nature of all things
In the black and white good and bad world
Frothing like a seizure

In dreams of loving boys and girls they cut me open

Pull out my brain knotted up from heat and inflammation

Friction from the desire to be good and
The hidden knowledge
This world is not as it should be
Is not at all what it appears to be

When I die they cut me open
Find a knot of axons in my lobes
The knot is the knot
They cut out

Of my DADDY's brain on some future date unknown
Before or after they cut me open
I had a dream they cut him open, shot protons through his skull
Found all along it wasn't madness

A delusion is an idea you let root in your soil
Born of and raised by two men whose error was certainty
I have never let certainty root in me
The boy is rooted, writhing on the pyre

[The brute. Brute heart]

Bowed down toward ground
Now in supplication
Waiting for some unlikely angel
To appear to us anon and intervene

RED FOOTBALL

If the *target memory* appears at all,
It's more of a composite image:
A tall man yelling, a toddler
Face down in a grey couch cushion
A handprint on his right ass cheek
Spreading red like shame
Or mildew, then melting into
The endorphins that
Always come to rescue pain

Whether or not this memory is *real*
No longer is concerning me

I had to learn to like it
If I was to survive it

I did both.

METANOIA

But my madness with myself was part of the process of recovering health...
—Augustine, *Confessions*, viii (19)

Charlotte,
Matisse wrote that to paint a rose one must
Forget every other rose painted first.
So fuck the roses. Who has the time. I ought to be
Asking more difficult questions like:
Where does my mental health end
And the planet's mental health begin?
It's stupid to write about flowers *qua* flowers.
They're not a fertile subject.
Five days of waking angry
Enough to strangle Morrissey
Watching my former idols
Immolate themselves for my education
Watching the Jenga blocks of my life
Wobble in a sexy and seductive way.
I despair only of myself.
Ecosystem and civilizational collapse
Is not how the newspapers read explicitly
But I have made a lifetime's work of
Reading between lines.
I came to the botanical gardens
To make myself feel at peace with
Sharing this place with an
Errant yellow jacket, my lifelong nemesis
Convincing myself that this suffering I feel
Is also a gift and that
Pain seems essential to revelation.
The magnolias are spectacular, Charlotte.
I wish that you were here to see them.
A storm of blight and being and ruin

In attractive guise of substance and form
Yellow as piss and pink as blood
Beauty you can watch rot in real time
If you're not doing much with your day.
Sometimes flowers are so beautiful
They make me want to kill myself, Charlotte.
I don't know why you killed yourself
Because we were barely friends
And hadn't spoken since high school
But I am not above admitting
I've thought about it
Three hundred times at least myself.
T. Liem wrote
Not these exact words
But close enough:
The poet
Can make absolutely anything
About absolutely anybody
About themself and thereby
Make it about everybody
If only for a moment.
I'm sitting in a wooden chair
Having my Augustine turning-
Outward-in-the-garden moment
Writing my second attempt
At making your life about mine, Charlotte.
Until four weeks ago, I'd been
a lifelong atheist. I can't tell if this feeling
That I'm feeling is
Me experiencing the presence of the Godhead in life
As my great-grandmother did and wrote about
Or if I'm having my first psychotic episode
As my father did instead

Or if there is a difference between the two.
What I do know:
The magnolias drop their comically large petals
Around my feet and in my feelings of despair
The Godhead or whatever
Has sent a cardinal
And a red-winged blackbird
To alight among the magnolia
Branches in front of me
A coincidence I interpret as a symptom
Of the hope I need to cradle in myself
If I hope to make it out of life alive.
Is this a meaningless coincidence
Or is it evidence of some design?
The worst thing about losing your mind
Is that your mind degrades
More or less exactly how
You expect it to
When you think of *losing your mind*
As if you're following a script
Somebody else wrote
Proving your brain is really not
That original or special. But then again you know that
Life can be cruel in this same way.
Sina told me tears are cheap in poetry but
I've found the cost I pay for crying's rather steep.
It's important to me that I be honest with you, Charlotte,
That I'm losing my mind
While listening to schmaltzy pop
Tears are streaming down my face
Torso rippling with gooseflesh
Brain imbalanced by certain chemicals
Feeling and seeing a connection

To an order of being and knowing
Something larger than myself
For the first time.
My great-grandmother wrote of it as
Beholding the glory of all things: every leaf
Every blossom, every particle of air glittering like a
Gem with its own fire.
Charlotte, I needed to survive you to behold it.
I wish that things were not this way
But know that no one
Can change how things were
Or how they will be
They only describe the way things are
And how things feel.
Right now it feels that life and death
Wasps and flowers
And God and puny me
Are one and the same: an unimaginable
Uncountable intelligence
Experiencing being through itself.
I needed to survive you
And to read every book that I had read
See everything that I had seen
Think everything that I had thought
To know it, to know it surely
As to know that my own feet
Lead me down the primrose path
To hell or madness or salvation
I do not know if what I feel or think
Flows from some ~ Spiritus Mundi ~ shit
The everlasting universe of things
A fallen angel, the cannabis I've vaporized
My genetic predisposition to nervous complaint

Dopamine flooding my synapses
Coupled with poor life choices
A tendency toward calculated risk.
I'm trying to let you know, Charlotte
Because you aren't here right now
Exactly how it feels
Down to the neurotransmitters
To the wax of the magnolia's petals
As though I'm knowing
God = death = life = void
In the flight of this cardinal and this blackbird
While also fearing I'm losing my grip
Though I'm not even the ten thousandth
White man wearing glasses
To feel this holy mania
Not even the first in my own family
To commit these thoughts to
Words; I am the son to my half-
Estranged unmedicated DADDY
Whose individual reality diverged
From consensus reality some years ago.
But what is poetry if not psychosis
With a little practice in enjambment and end rhyme.
What is poetry but seeing
The cardinal alight on the magnolia
Knowing the beauty of
The bird and branch
Rest in this transience
The passing from flower into rot
The bird from bloom to earth
Inseparable from my joy
At the sight or scent
Of petals dropping to the ground

Or the cardinal singing a sweet
Ditty that reminds me
Spring hopes garish and floridly
The cardinal's flight my anchor
Between what is real and knowable and not
Among the living and the dying magnolias
God has either sent me
Or has not, trembling before the
Fact that somehow
I got tasked with deciding which
Picture of the facts aligns with how it is.
Stopping to smell roses
Cumming on my stomach
Reading a dead man's theology and
Women for how to live in grace
During the Anthropocene
Living off usury from future generations
Shitting my pants in fear of something I can't name
Doubting, because my middle name is Thomas, but
Knowing I can see the Godhead in these flowers, Charlotte
That my life has taught me what I need to know to tell you that
Though you are not here and these birds
And flowers are
I can smell their lemony
Salami odour, I can watch petals fall
Backwards and forwards through time
I can find a beauty in their suffering
Just as I can—and—do in mine

A POEM ABOUT MY PET CANARY II

I have to assume her intentions were noble.
Maybe I don't like to accept the alternative.

I know the bird sat dead for hours,
              and I know she knew that
well before she yelled us down for supper.

I know the bird's name—Sunny—has not been spoken since.

I know I took my usual seat
at the perfect vantage
to have seen
his scaly legs stick upwards
from the bottom
of the shit-encrusted cage.

I wanted desperately to
run to my bunk
so I could cry
for the yellow bird I'd killed
because I failed to do my chores.

I was made to sit and finish every bite of dinner.

When I tried to cry that night
I could not, found only
a numb grey fuzz
in the part of my chest
where emotions ought to be.
I interpreted this numbness
as proof of my monstrosity,
shut down for fear of the feelings, their immensity,
that should they ever be displayed

Mommy and DADDY wouldn't love me,
that things were better off that way,
heart encased in patina of bird shit,
cauterized and callused hard.

My parents taught me many things the hard way.

But I cannot for the life of me recall
what the moral of this lesson was.

Do poems require moral lessons?

If there is one, it's that
even though she took me
to the pet shop two weeks later
to watch her sell the cage back
to the owner on consignment, that
even though by then I'd seen
three or four family pets disappear already,
even though the bird wasn't even
the first of these I'd had to watch,
some part of me inside
believes it's all my fault.
At seven already a bird-murderer.

One day I hope to forgive myself.

MADNESS

Capital flowed from me
Faster than it ought to,
That's true.
I guess I spoke a bit
Faster than usual, and
I'm sure friends and family
Would agree I hadn't previously
Been interested in the religious
Philosophies of Hinduism,
Or crystals, or reiki.
The spring my book came out
My cat, the creature I held
Most dear in all the world,
Was dying young, satisfying
The catalytic requirement of
Stressful life circumstances.
There's nature: my father has the disorder, or one of them.
And nurture: I blasted my own brain
With drugs, lots of them, from an early age
In order to cope with the
Childhood one associates with phrases like
Early life adversity or
Affectionless control.
Given these many, many
Variables, all outlaid in
The Fifth Edition of the
Diagnostic and Statistical Manual of Mental Disorders,
If we were to look upon
Impartial observer or an
Intaking clinician,
Or look upon it
From the inside
As *the* impartial observer,

We might be able to say
In a certain regard
That mania, my family's
And my father's madness,
Had finally come for me at last.
                What I hadn't expected
In the years that I watched for it
Like an orchid fiend for boll weevils or
Hawk swooping over prairie
I guess somewhere in my heart
I did expect it would feel good,
Fucking amazing, I guess, better than
Any high a chemical could induce—
You can trust me, I've induced all of 'em—
Because if it hadn't felt good, my father
Might not have chosen madness over me.
What I didn't expect
When I moved through my life
Is that when mania came for me
I would fall into it, willingly
Like I could fall into
A hadal zone or waterbed,
That in the depths of my fall
I'd dissolve there, just
Like I was rock salt poured into
A pot of boiling water, or like
The Joker falling backwards
Into a vat of acid.
After it came for me, and this is the
Worst part—I hadn't expected
It would feel like *the truth*

gnostic
iambic
pre-exposure
jockstrap
jukebox
prophylaxis

I don't know, I don't know.
After one kiss the world's quite changed.
—Ko Un, "A Traveller's Loneliness"

having recently been pissed in

by a man whose name i didn't ask
but called the same name i call my stepfather
i strolled into the formless night alone

knock-knock joke

impossible not
feel frisson of joy
when cardinal flies
or animal control guy's
butt soooo amazing in the corduroys
his head up chimney
scaring birds. two years today
saw bird fly into tree
wept because i thought a god moved
through it and then through me.
like a jewel [burning] *with its own fire*
on day when else is brown and blue and grey

sumac grows through pavement
beside chlorinated public pool
in which no one swims

can you trust
        the blood that races through your heart?
        how do you know?

have you ever seen it run?

saturday night's alright for fisting

whatever i did to deserve
The Phantom of the Opera earwormed
on my commute to work
i renounce. locust bean pods
rotting underfoot. soggy cigarette
butts   curtain of cleansing rains   street lights
full moon
in pavement puddles
trying to consecrate the images in time
from the weekend at the bathhouse   so sing for me
angel of ~~music +~~ memory ;)
ed said he wasn't on the path he saw for himself at thirty
the path on which a muscle twunk named ed with cum gutters
blue eyes   many people would die for, if not me
gives me the time of day   forcefully
into my uvula
that's not the path i saw for myself either
and the price i pay for it is dear
my brain screaming
can you not see i am unlovable
unfuckable?
in the pornography viewing room   throngs of men   a lightning bolt
chaining through our navels   chemicals singing   coloratura in our bodies
this is the desire that others us   unites us secure in our desires
one multitude, one purpose
the games we play in here
the straight world gives no credit for
they do not understand what it means
to say you walk the forking path   how old were you
when you first saw that time
was just a shadow on a wall?
how long have i sat vigil here
at the altar of the god who comes

who promises the experience a human life can bear
so long as you surrender utterly to it
naked, sweat-drunk, on the maenads' vine
the hole without that leads within   the world that
enters it by will
the way i give myself to it
the agapé of all my brothers at the orgy
the love of god or man
swelling, threatening to bust
to kool-aid man right through
the four walls of the blasted world
the object i call me   the subject i call you

polyamorous love song

my second boyfriend's husband's boyfriend

pulls the page of cups

we love the only way we should:

ecstatically

under the red light

concrete floor wet with verruca and lube

i composed this poem while david fucked me

i then apologized for not remaining present with him

in mind, if still in body

what are these lights in us

decaying as we move

further from our souce?

who told me this was wrong?

the sensation of air

passing into lungs

from my ribs into

his and his

and his?

perhaps they ought to fear us faggots after all

go back to party city where you belong

you were born for this, you little faggot.
—some guy named tony, to me, april 2019

the thing is, tony wasn't wrong

subwoofer singing through my body

jockstrap under these dancing pants

feeling like imminent civilizational collapse

last-rooftop-pool-party-in-Weimar kinda vibe

i guess that makes me a decadent

but i thought before i have to let it go

i'd get to know my body intimately

guzzle champagne and cum

learn how to to love myself   offline

how to love myself while choking up phlegm, crying

my back pressed against a wall

or trawling the internet again for cock five hours later

this is healthy. this is individuation

tony, maybe i was born to meet you

maybe we were meant to dance all night

the universe brings me my bedfellows

I hunt when the moon's full   I sleep through the light

in the steam room of the young men's christian association

hello, older gentleman
not my DADDY
but you could be my DADDY
another universe away
sudsing your body in the public change room shower
a little longer than is necessary
infusing soap with subtle auras
only men like me
and those who fuck the men like me
possess the antenna to pick up
among the grout
the inexpressive smoothness of the tile
the beige on cream
the high c hiss of towel steam
the icy treble of bromine
the smile
the secret sign
the quickening of blood
the collapsing star of my open hole
your fingers guiding something
from without within me
something knowable
yet still unseen

the brotherhood of the forking path

O Lord, make me chaste, but not yet!
—Augustine, *Confessions*, viii (7)

there's a sort of wistfulness gay men excel at
if we weren't just passing through ourselves
via each other's bodies tonight
we'd be companions in another life
they'd sing songs about the love we had, if we had any
but all the love we have is here before us now
a bond made sacred by fluid exchange, a sacrament—
something mystic we cannot name

the brotherhood of the forking path:
those who aim to know themselves
grab a body to know themselves by
as they pass another, moving
thousands of kilometres per second
in opposite directions, the leader
and the return stroke, one toward
earth that birthed us, the other toward heaven
lighting what is possible
faster than an eye can see
gravity wobbling, lensing
passing in the endless night of space
two entities (or three or more)
celebrate a temporary victory
over death's grim kingdom
in a flash

in another life
in another world
i'm going to love you to death
but not yet

bugged life

i   like to think of them as my wages   for sin
or the labours that I did for love
taking my pants off for doctors   coats unblemished as their morals
a lot of   *i don't know why you guys need to be having*
all that sex
six-inch needles in the glutes
beads of blood on finger pricks
and frequent swabs of rectum and of throat
cultures grown from life inside me
lice shampoo that leaves a bitter taste
an identifiable characteristic of pyrethroids
a spare in the bathroom just in case
bugs have always loved me   my honeyed blood
rushing to   my face
my   stupid   sexy   brain

event coordinator moving into project management

sometimes you know
by the crackle of static in the air
the vibrations in the puddles
on the sopping sauna floor.
i had so rarely felt the virtues of a
tall white man before marco.
an event coordinator *looking to move into*
project management—i don't know how to talk
to people with real jobs—he spent his days
an ersatz priest officiating weddings
(italian, bearded, i look the part)
in this place that's all about appearances. there is a love i have
            for the blasted world that leaks
            from my body hot and wet
            in a tiled room choked
            with eucalyptus steam
            red light, hyperpyretic piping
            when every orifice of mine is full
            with the warm promise of tomorrow

amuse douche

when my trachea is blocked
and i forget to breathe
through my imperfect human septum
and the bile rises into my throat
when the acid of my stomach admixes with your juices
and my spit and phlegm
when i'm skinning my knees on the concrete
when i'm doing the lord's work

then

operation desert stave

i'm interested to know how one becomes...
ex-head of hair colour...purchasing?   for l'oréal tokyo by twenty-seven
but not interested enough...
the sting of shame
and want for cash   in my lifestyle choices
what humiliating degradations maxime would bark at me in french
if i let him   but why would i ever again fuck a man in his twenties
still learning how to cock his walk?
there is a certain beauty about maxime   i don't tend to go for "beautiful"
his station begs to me   a question
would i   abandon what i loved   all that i professed to believe
were they merely dependent on my context   and environment
would i appear in the fabulous metropole where   capitalism seemed a little kinder
or its viciousness was   concealed from me   by a language barrier
could i live like that
in a state of denial   loins comfortable in silks and rayons
hairs on my asshole snuggled in   high thread count cotton
such beautiful things

such beautiful things

love to be

long to be   free

my tragedy

for abhi

i just spent the night
with the most beautiful boy
smile lit up my room
when he was inside
i felt union
with god

some faiths conceive of desire as a wheel
keeping us bound here in realms of illusion
or like popular carnival attraction *the zipper*
bashing your skull on the cage as you whirl

but my tragedy:
the most beautiful boy
i've yet seen in this life—
the new one—
has just told me his name
as his husband spins
next to us on a barstool chair
and i am sliiightly flexing
every muscle in my body
so that i'm leaning, subtly
into the hungry curve
of his deltoid and pectoral muscles, so that
if an onlooker were watching
i would appear to be swaying
into the centre of his orbit
one breath away from contact
while still firmly on my feet
like a moon around a planet
my cycle thus again complete

lacy lesions forming

where the polyurethane cage
in which i've locked my cock
chafes against my sweaty

hairy thighs. never could
keep my hands to myself
or from myself, specifically

in bondage may you
set your trembling
rabbit heart free

like how some
imagine the mechanism
by which

a gemstone
"works," by sopping up
ambient energy

or a stein
filled to brim
overflowing with head

counterintuitive
but by now i know
to relinquish control

is how i control myself
effectively
how does someone

become securely attached
by any way other than
fastening?

pornography taught
early, hot but
poor facsimile

of desire and love
but better than my
catholic education on

the practices and principles of buggery
and if i am to choose between hellfire or
chastity, i say why not both?

control
and denial
are the only

hammers in my box of tools
that got me halfway
living where i

want to be
there is no lock
and key that could secure

my rabbit heart from quickening
time-honoured skirmish
of predator/prey

how some boys long to be good
but cannot for inside they are naughty
flesh expanding, capillaries swelling with

I think I fucked up   my desire
to squeeze my whole life
into the tensile confines of poetry

folie à deux

abhi told me he could imagine no reality
outside his direct perception, then smiled and said
he must have imagined me into being, atom to atom

well, it's not my first time dancing
tarantella with a man
who saw me merely as a vessel for his input

it's also a completely insane thing to say to somebody
on a second date, which endears him to me greatly
and so i swallow fear and go ahead

lines composed after getting fucked by a hypnotist

for kyle

the world is ending; i accept this.
i gulp it up. i take it deeper into me
than any hand has gone before or since.
today a man fed me a slice of oblivion
and smeared sweet airy meringue
all over the skull i mistook for my face.
all over these words as empty as wombs.
my mother's, specifically—
the ache of that wound. and yet my body
did hide it away for me, in a pocket i
or another man could open up
if i ever felt relaxed or safe,
lined with leather, a flesh
made supple in death by chemicals,
reeking of birch tar and jasmine.
i no longer fear the pain that is cached there.
i draw breath like you might a sword
pulled out a sheath, over and over,
again back and forth.

edging

on the precipice of a terrible moment in history

i turned toward a screen

i hated the derisory tone of the word *screen*

as i loved and hated the screens themselves

but like *being alive in the present*

i had no suitable alternatives

my worth was quantifiable: i reduced myself

into syrup

down to essences net worth

data biometrics

i texted him *i'm too depressed to fuck*

he said *sorry to hear that but*

i can't wait to lick your hole again ☺

dude read the room

i ghosted whatever joke's on me

the hole was my entire mind and body

two weeks later he followed me

into a convenience store and down my street

i thus resolved my fitness goals: to become unapproachable

to become

qualia   ejecta   corporate responsibility

a commitment to diversity

histamine-seared   a ring in an ear
a broken cascade

of lysosomes   a ring of shaggy inkcaps

the wisdom hid in mycelia we never learned

on the crank of widened gyre

DADDY didn't love them
so they fell in love with tyrants
DADDY didn't love me
so i fell on my knees
for his deputies, lieutenants
his acting subsidiaries

mother couldn't hold me though she tried
so i sought her breasts in drugs and candy
and i liked it
i liked it like that
we all did   we were living
in a narrative we did not understand

there were ICBMs suspended in the air

there were notifications pending

gleaming in the glass   but there were also autumn leaves

glinting gold and rotting in the pass

there was a logic to it i couldn't grasp

when i tore it up on the dance floor

in my lycra fetish wear

when i stomped my feet

when i shook my ass

a jester in the court of love at midnight in the hellfire realms

for andrew

once i got a little
i wanted a lot.
then i got a lot
and still i wanted little else.
a very hungry ghostly little
caterpillar squirmed within
my anus, devouring all
that i'd feed to it
and how i'd feed it;
and how i do.
i wanted to sing
every tune in the hymnal,
until my voice was cracked and hoarse.
i believed if i stayed till the end of the ceremony
i might discover
something new to say about life,
beyond the creak of the bed,
or the farting noise when my skin unstuck from yours
after you took your beautiful torso off of mine.
have i ever told you
that you have a beautiful torso?
have you ever felt
a man's beautiful desire adhere
to the shape of your own
from across the bookstore, the hot tub,
the half-full subway car?
have you ever
been given instructions
to sneak in the back, past
the red-painted gate, up
the wrought-iron staircase

and the sliding glass door
after his husband is asleep?
have you ever felt a need
superseding every other?
what was the need, and
where did you feel it
in your body? have you
ever taken your place
as jester in the court of love
at midnight in the hellfire realms?
of course you have, you bad thing, you.
have you ever danced a pas de deux
with shoes soled red as licking flames?
what desires will you walk over coals for?
can you hear them now hollering,
chanting your name?

LONG POEM II

The everlasting universe of things
Flows through the mind, and rolls its rapid waves
—Shelley, "Mont Blanc: Lines Written in the Vale of Chamouni"

Lone persimmon
Bruised under the fruit stall at night

The sweetness of childhood
Turns to rotting fruit

Tureens of
sweet whipped cream

Midway upon the fitness journey   of my   life
I found myself alone

This was the   opening
Of my   long poem

"Long Poem II"

This is how it opened

Like spirea, white flowers
Clustered like staph
In the
Back of a throat
Swollen shut

And the reader
Seeking an entrance into
The   poem

The world was ending, slowly

It was the fifth heat wave of the
Fifth consecutive hottest summer on record
I happened to have been born
And been alive at
Kind of a weird time in history

The end of society, maybe?
The music's only just started
I have excellent seats to the show

But it was summertime

Every human that
I passed looked smoking hot
Their tans
Their exposed flesh
Their loose-fitting garments

Everyone
I passed had already lost a lot
Were going to lose more
Than they could bear or dedicate to words

My friends and
I laughing in the August sun

I am here
In my floral one-piece
Left partially unbuttoned
In Vancouver, a city where negative attention
Seems too easy to come by
I am here with my people
We are all happy and warm and smiling
We are all doing our very best

Two teenage boys on a Vespa whiz by

This was the *rising action* of my long poem
Long Poem II
Normally these things
Were supposed to have a narrative arc

I declined
I had other aims in mind

Too interested
In the whims of gods
Reflected in the tide's steady lap lap lap
As the moon waxes sinister Hot concrete belch
There on the horizon Cascade of cool herbaceous air

A heart pierced by an iron spear
Emblazoned with a golden crown

I have this fantasy, you see
In it I live to a ripe old age
But not too old Still
my body's wracked with aches
And I'm dying of an inoperable cancer. Anyway
I'm in my beautiful coastal pied-à-terre
Even though I've never liked the beach I'm dying
Surrounded by the ones I love though I've chosen not to sire
A family

Or was that chosen for me? My linen-lined deathbed
Soft vignette lighting mid-century modern furniture
I've travelled just enough haven't seen
All the world, just enough to feel contented by

Ugh

What's the fucking point?
My generation's doomed

We've all got
Apocalypse syndrome
Autoimmune disorders gastrointestinal complaints

Okay that's
The fantasy I die relatively content
Relatively painlessly
Even with all this damage that I'm doing to my butthole
With saline enemas
Sat on luxury toilets with bidet attachments
Heated seats
Whooshing air

The trees do marvel in the whooshing air

Tawny star of his hair

That's not the
World I live in man

It's hard to face the summer sun
When this melancholy seizes me
When I tire even

Of

Shopping and fucking

What is the name for

The discipline of the
Study of

The blight at the heart of a family?

Psychology

The blight at the heart of a species?

Poetry

Is thinking about God psychosis?

Is thinking about God a rational response
To a world whose cruelty and ugliness
Just to witness those two powers
Has cut me to the bone?

All my life I'd been an atheist

I pass through the twin smokestacks on Rue St. Émile
By which I orient my route demarcating
Experience and reason real
And unreal
Rigour and mercy

Enter Unto His Gates With Thanksgiving

In the neon-scented paradise of shopping
I find myself alone

The humiliation   of the sales rack watching
Top brands of yesterday
Fail to command their perceived value
Feeling a sort of pity for a brand

Walking through the city that is my life
Thinking of what to buy   and
How to raise the capital to buy it

Soirees and galas

I'm sorry, I don't have any change

Waiting for   an inalienable sign
From the kingdom and palace   of   life
Concrete belching out   our passions it has absorbed
In the form and constant   of heat

But here are trees in bloom
How is it I had gone my whole life never seeing
Trees in bloom

Till high horse chestnut   spanning aeons

Wind brings no relief to August
What time my generation had was spent before my birth

This world is an aleph
Should you choose to look

In August heat

You can view the suffering of those
You could call kin
If not for accident of birth or fate

Why must we continue this project of history?
Why must we ride this line to its terminus
Drugged
And dropped into discriminate units
Our blood transfigured into gold

Still

You need to be primed
For moments of serendipitous beauty
In this life

Take what you can get

Look!
This world has exactly enough
Space for you to live in it

Hope is a yoke
You carry for others
Isn't it

Saying
I hope you have a nice day
To a service-industry employee

It isn't good enough

Weigh my heart against the feather
I saw in a video
Of an albatross choking
On a gullet full of plastic
My takeout containers
My fast and free shipping
My disposable razors

Under a crushing magistrate
Hunger carries me into night

Hunger carries me

In the sweaty post-workout cock
Of the lily
Bitten lip of rose

I am a human being and thus I have two drives
Desire and the
Desire not to die
Tonight my fear of my own death is a man
I desire
My fear of my own death puts his collar on my neck
Tonight
I am his *hole*
I smell turpentine
My fear of my own death points to the concrete floor
I put my face there

My fear of my own death
Pulls out his

At three a.m. in the bathhouse a High-NRG
remix of Evanescence's "My Immortal"
Comes on as
I huff amyl nitrate
This is unfortunately my *Mont Blanc* moment

I'm just another page the reader's writing a poem on

I wish my desire were revolutionary
I wish my desire could inspire revolutions
My desire will not revolt
In real time my desire will revolt you

Born into the realm of ravenous ghosts
The reader's open hole
In this red light a nebula collapsing
I devour all information that approaches
My event horizon

And still I thought Yeah This is personhood
And still I thought This is the good shit

Pre-workout supplement
Post-workout chicken and broccoli This is it!
The nerve endings surrounding
My asshole
That's all there is !!!
In this shopping mall of tears

When my consciousness departs my body
And rejoins Death slash God
All I'll report is
Shopping and fucking
The love I once had
For the purr of a kitten

As a child I scorned those
Who relied on the fantasy of a benevolent deity
To face the hardships of a world
Governed seemingly only by callousness and chance

By the time I was thirty was so tired I was like

You know what? gimme the fantasy

I neeeed the fantasy

Waiter, I will have what he's having!

Which if rephrased in
Poet Voice
Might go a little something like
But that mortal terror was
To unfurl inside me also... carnivorous pomegranate...
Flash-frozen pink chrysanthemum... tears in winter rain...

Passing a taco restaurant at night a Patrick Bateman–type in navy
three-piece suit
Adjusts his blue silk tie in front
Of
A garish painting of a clown

Life constantly
Demanding I accept the burden of its absurdity

This world needed to change
But the only thing I'd ever been able to change
Is myself
With great effort

My long poem Long Poem II
Has been
In need of
A narrative
A narrative by which to thread a camel through a rich man's eye
To connect these abstract concepts
In a way that remains universal and relatable

But what to give you God or reader
I have not
Given you already?
The night I was assaulted?
I've given you that before buried
Seven layer dip in metaphor *Tawny star of his hair* I was nineteen
Being groomed by a local *activist*
It's funny to see photos of him pop up on the feeds of friends
New cities his hairline recedes further
And the teenagers he's surrounded by
Stay the same age don't they?

He sold me a lot of ecstasy
Which I gladly licked out of the bag

I wouldn't recommend but neither do regret those poor decisions
Although the memories from that iconic era
Do invoke in me
An involuntary shiver

I made some friends
I had some fun
I learned a lot about myself and built some character

I try to take responsibility for
What I can

Even the things that were not
My fault

Perhaps those things
Especially

To do so gives me a sensation
Of control
In a system whose complexity is unintelligible to me

Date rape, or something you might have sort
Of wanted to do at the time with someone else
But absolutely not like that Tawny star
Of his hair
My crown bleeding on the concrete wall

Not in that way

Not so drunk

I couldn't walk

Or how it felt to realize later

How many other boys
It has been going on to

Are you okay
Are you okay, Ali?
There's a player piano

A crescendo Ali

A doctor gave me a white and oblong pill
All my life I'd been an atheist
And now thought I could hear God whispering
Through shapes and symbols I perceive

There was something larger in the mystery I'd need

A phenomenon
Older than I could name
Or had words for

Who wears the bones of the past as a yoke?
The earth demands and
You only have a moment to collect your things and go

I claim *yes* that is me
I shall face myself on the threshold
And I shall not look away

These are the feelings, ideas, and sensations
That close out
My long poem
Long Poem II

Everything I could

Put to words
There was a power in words still

I could feel that power
On the day I learned to write

I took that power in
My hands and

Placed it onto a sheet of tan unbleached paper

My junior kindergarten teacher pulled from a wheel in strips

Mrs. Barber, a kindly woman, my memory of whom
I cannot disentangle

From that of Lily Tomlin's   Ms. Frizzle—can you believe
                    Lily Tomlin was Ms. Frizzle all this time—
The paper

Tacked onto a large blue plastic easel
Affixed with coloured magnets shaped like letters
I took into my hands a coloured pencil

Scrawled the word *DRUM* onto the page

Took a step backwards   and thought

                    In my four-year-old brain

          Look on my works, ye Mighty, and despair!

                    In so many words, anyway

The feeling I've had so many times before
                                        And since
                    In   words
                    In dreams

That something of my life was going to change
Awe at the edge of the precipice
Between tomorrow and the day before

Reader, please commit the pen to paper

And in a substance made
Of words

I can say to you

Go then and tell them what you found

Written in blood in the book of yourself

Go and write it all of it

And then
I want you
To
Noting especially

The scent of sulfur

As you strike up the match on
The concrete wall

As the match lights into a tawny star

And then

Then I want you

To burn it

already this feeling of peace is departing me

after luis fucks me for hours
without breaking eye contact

when i take his cock
longer, harder than i have for any other man

when he makes my body bleed
and i look him in the eyes and thank him for it

buzzing with endogenous chemicals
that make me feel easy

i walk out into the eggplant night
feeling loose and sloppy

cum and lube dripping down my leg
soaking the upholstery of the streetcar

but so goes my attachment to suffering:
already this feeling of peace is departing me...

the devil reversed

cast off your chains
and be free. like it's easy. like it won't
cost you a damn thing. like
a damned thing is or is not.
like a damned thing thought.
like thought was the damnable act
and the thinking hell's reprise.
hell's reprise is thought skinned blue
in submission and in servitude.
about the sublimation of the will
i think i know a thing or two.
a quiet pocket to let the obedient child
nest into, where they feel safe and secure,
warm and embraced. love is a law
and hell is a place. hell is a place
where we all hold the keys.
let love do the thinking.
get down on your knees.

the court of love

as christopher was
absolutely pummelling luca into the mattress
and madhur was fondling
luca's hair as christopher did it, giving
luca sweet words of encouragement, and yuen,
first timer to an orgy, was touching pete's cock
as pete was sucking howard, then kysan, then fox
as stephen only came to watch
as richard nuzzled his scruff in my shoulder, it was then
i turned to him and said,
if there exists a paradise on earth, this is it

poem for "aaron"

BLUE LIGHT
BLUE LIGHT
BLUE LIGHT   yellow

not me
falling in love again
on a tuesday   !!!

i wasn't focused on the hands
of the other men
who grabbed my
thighs as "aaron" fucked me
on the sauna's public pommel horse.
i was focused on the little ring of muscle
two centimetres inside my rectum, relaxing
and tightening it in a cyclical rhythm.
once, then again. gay sex got way easier
once i started meditating.
i wasn't focused on
the hands of the men, i was focused on
keeping my back straight and low,
with my glutes engaged, to prevent
spasm and injury tomorrow
and to provide leverage
for aaron's pleasure. he's
not the first to have given me
a pseudonym, i'm sure. i was
focused on aaron pulling out
so he could cum inside my throat.
cum down my throat
on an empty stomach
inevitably makes me yak.
i showered, then i walked outside

and saw the moon, who has
witnessed so much human suffering
and still says nothing, unless you listen
very, very carefully. i walked outside
with aaron, with whom i was
falling in love again on a tuesday
and whom i will likely never see again.
i saw the moon complete
its cycle round the earth
and now my revolution begins again.

NOTES, REFERENCES, INFLUENCES

The opening epigraphs are from *The Collected Poems of Audre Lorde* (W.W. Norton, 2000) and from David Lynch's 1997 film *Lost Highway.*

PARALLEL VOLUMES

The "paraphrase" of Dionne Brand comes from the first section of *The Blue Clerk* (McClelland & Stewart, 2019).

"Pilot the Eva, Shinji, or Rei will have to do it again" cites a meme describing a scene from the first episode of *Neon Genesis Evangelion*.

Borges's library is, of course, his library of Babel.

The final page paraphrases Alan Watts' advice for psychedelic drug users from *The Joyous Cosmology: Adventures in the Chemistry of Consciousness* (New World Library, 2013), advising, "When you get the message, hang up the phone."

EERIE HONEY

The first draft of this poem was composed in a "chatbox jam" (exquisite corpse, Zoom-style) at Filip Marinovich's *Motley* Shakespearian College. Many thanks to Filip.

DADDY

"I—I could love myself, instead!!!" quotes the English subtitles for ADV Film's dub of Episode 25 of *Neon Genesis Evangelion.*

Super Smash Bros. Party Ball refers to an item found in Nintendo's popular *Super Smash Bros.* franchise of video games.

INTIMACY

This poem quotes Goldberg's Aug 31, 2016 interview with *The New York Times Magazine*, conducted by Ana Marie Cox.

PORTION

Self-compassion is a Buddhist concept popularized in mainstream Western psychology by Dr. Kristin Neff of University of Texas, Austin.

GAMES NIGHT!!!

Boggle and Risk are trademarks belonging to Hasbro.

II OF RODS

The Ashton Kutcher movie in question is *The Butterfly Effect* (Eric Bress and J. Mackye Gruber, 2004). Not worth seeing if you haven't.

"Sometimes my arms bend back" quotes Episode 3 of Season 1 of *Twin Peaks* (Mark Frost and David Lynch, 1990).

Final Fantasy X belongs to Square Enix.

Spy vs Spy was a long-running cartoon in *Mad Magazine.*

"A kindling pyre in the mountains of Moriah" is my highfalutin' paraphrase of *Genesis* 22: 2, NKJV.

"The brute. Brute heart" belongs to Sylvia Plath's "Daddy" from *Ariel* (Faber & Faber, 1965).

RED FOOTBALL

This poem steals its title from a song by Sinead O'Connor.

METANOIA

The Matisse paraphrase comes from an artist's statement he wrote in 1954, which was republished for the 2014 Matisse retrospective at The Tate Modern.

This poem paraphrases T. Liem's "Anonymous woman elegy", from *Obits* (Coach House Books, 2018).

The line "But then again you know that" parrots a line of dialogue spoken by Tilda Swinton's character Karen Crowder in the film *Michael Clayton* (Tony Gilroy, 2007)

The quote written by my great-grandmother, Norah Holden Pilkington, is contained in *Sights and Insights*, Vol. 2, her memoir, compiled and self-published by my grandmother, Isabel Henniger.

*

The epigraph for *gnostic iambic pre-exposure jockstrap jukebox prophylaxis* is Ko Un's from *Songs for Tomorrow: Poems 1961-2001* (Green Integer, 2009).

saturday night's alright for fisting

The title riffs on Elton John's "Saturday Night's Alright for Fighting".

"The god who comes" is an epithet for Dionysus.

polyamorous love song

The title belongs to Jacob Wren's novel *Polyamorous Love Song* (Book*hug Press, 2014).

lacy lesions forming

"Why not both" is the Taco Bell commercial made into an ubiquitous early 2010s Internet meme, which is by now rather ancient.

lines composed after getting fucked by a hypnotist

"I gulp it up" is the *second* time a poem of mine has quoted the film *There Will Be Blood* (Paul Thomas Anderson, 2008), and writing these notes is making me keenly aware my pop culture references require an update.

a jester in the court of love at midnight in the hellfire realms

The Court of Love refers to the one apocryphally run by Eleanor of Aquitane in the 12th century CE.

There are red-soled shoes here, so that's Kate Bush, Hans Christian Andersen, and the movie with the same name that I've never seen.

LONG POEM II

"Midway upon the journey of my life" is Dante, *Inferno*, Canticle 1.

"Enter Unto His Gates With Thanksgiving" is text I read off the entrance to a church near Gare Centrale in Montreal, QC.

"Shopping mall of tears" belongs to perfume writer Luca Turin.

The "aleph" referenced is Borges's.

"Weigh my heart against a feather" is pop-culture Egyptian mythology.

Patrick Bateman is a character from Bret Easton Ellis's novels, that I must stress I last enjoyed when still a teenager.

"Camel through a needle's eye," riffed on here, is NKJV Matthew 19:24.

Page 125 riffs on Michael Jackson's "Smooth Criminal" (1998).

SPECIAL THANKS TO

Everyone at Brick Books, everyone at Wolsak & Wynn, Kilby Smith-McGregor, Canisia Lubrin, Ali Pinkney, John Barton, River Halen Guri, Kysan Kwan, Abhijith Ponnan, Filip Marinovich, Ariana Reines, Ben Ladouceur, Kess Mohammadi, my family, Cassidy McFadzean, Daniel Zomparelli, Adèle Barclay, Luis Galvão, the Canada Council for the Arts, the Ontario Arts Council, Graeme Lamb, and David Burrows.

Thanks to the editors and publishers of the following journals in which this work has appeared or is forthcoming: Metatron Press, *guest* magazine, *Glyphoria*, *echolocation*, *Best Canadian Poetry 2022*, *Plenitude*, *Grain*, *CV2*, and *underblong*.

JAKE BYRNE lives in Toronto.